COMP

2. HEAD FIRST

Text by Barbara Cooper

Illustrations by Maggie Raynor

Series consultant: Valerie Watson

Compass Equestrian

Setting by HGJ
Origination by Dot Gradations
Printed in England by Westway Offset

ISBN 1 900667 01 0

British Library Cataloguing in Publication Data.
A catalogue record for this book is available from the British Library.

A pony's head is widest across his forehead, and smallest down at his mouth and nose. On each side are big flat cheeks. By looking at a pony's head and face you can learn a great deal about him.

Ponies who come from cold areas such as Northern Britain and the Alps, have broad, strong heads with fan-shaped forelocks to protect their eyes from the rain, and long, coarse hair under their chins.

Ponies whose ancestors come from warmer climates such as that of Arabia have bonier heads, less hairy chins and more wide-awake eyes.

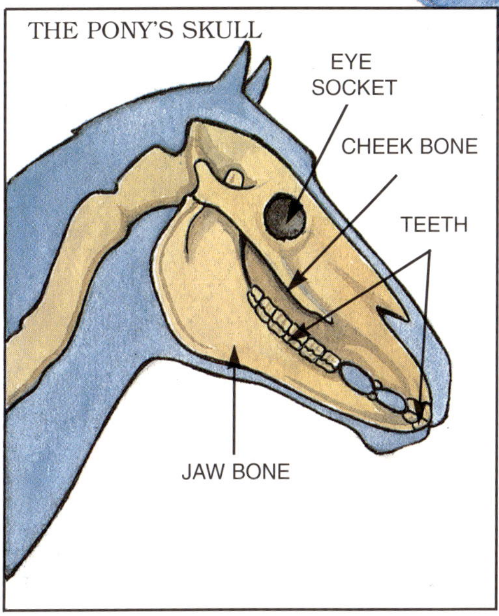

If you stroke a pony under his chin you can feel the soft area where his tongue lies between his two long jaw bones.

Unlike pigs, sheep and cows, ponies have long necks.

A pony uses his neck to balance himself (as a cat or a monkey uses its tail), and he stretches it out when he gallops and jumps.

Some ponies have beautifully-shaped necks, but others have ugly ones. If a pony's neck is not a nice shape it may be called a 'ewe neck' or a 'bull neck' or even a 'swan neck'. (A neck which is elegant on a swan is not at all elegant on a pony!)

You can tell a lot about a pony from his ears. Their shape and size are a useful guide to his character. For example, a happy pony whom you can trust will generally prick his ears forward most of the time.

Some ponies have big, generous ears

and some have small, sharp ones.

A pony's ears are constantly moving. Even when he puts his head down to drink, his ears flick to and fro listening for the sound of another creature (such as you) creeping up on him.

It is with his ears that a pony talks to you. On the next two pages you can learn the signals, or 'ear language'.

When both of a pony's ears are forward it means that he is happy, or has noticed something interesting or pleasing or even dangerous.

When one ear is back and the other is pointing upwards, it means that the pony is listening to you.

If his ears are floppy, the pony is feeling relaxed and happy.

In all three pictures here the ponies' ears are back.

This pony is very angry.

This pony is frightened.

This pony is not well.

Your eyes are set at the front of your face, so you can see ahead but you can't see behind without turning round.

A pony's eyes are set at each side of his face, so each eye can see separately. He can see to the front, and by raising and turning his head a little he can see behind as well.

If he needs to look closely at something he will turn his head or stretch out his neck so that he can use both eyes at once.

You can learn a lot about a pony by looking at his eyes. Some have large, gentle, honest eyes and others have small, piggy, mean ones.

A pony uses his nose not just to smell with but also to touch and feel. He uses his wide nostrils, not his mouth, to breathe through even when he is swimming.

When he has been galloping or jumping, his nostrils become even wider, and they quiver as he breathes.

Some ponies and horses put their noses right under the water when they are drinking, and they flatten their nostrils so that the water does not get into them.

A pony's muzzle (the area around his nostrils) is soft and velvety, with long whiskers which tickle when the pony snuffles you (touches you with his muzzle.)

His whiskers act as feelers and are as important to him as whiskers are to a cat.

Many ponies and horses have white or pink marks on their faces.

The mark may be ...

a star

a stripe

a blaze

a snip, and
a pink lip

a star, a stripe
and a pink nose

or
the
face may
be nearly
all white

Between his eyes you will see a patch of hair which grows in a circle like a wheel. This is called a 'whorl'. Ponies and horses also have whorls in other places such as on their chests and flanks.

Some ponies have a ring of cream-coloured hair around their eyes. This is called a 'toad eye'. If they have the same coloured hair on their noses, it is called a 'mealy muzzle'.

You may have noticed that we are on the last page of a book about heads without so much as a mention of a pony's brain-power.

Although your head is a lot smaller than that of an average-size pony, your brains are bigger, rounder and at least twice as heavy. This doesn't mean that ponies are not as smart as you. They may think and behave very differently, but their brains are just as busy as yours in their own way which you will find out in Book 8 of this series : 'Why does he do that?'

The book after this one tells you about a pony's body...which in some ways is surprisingly like yours.

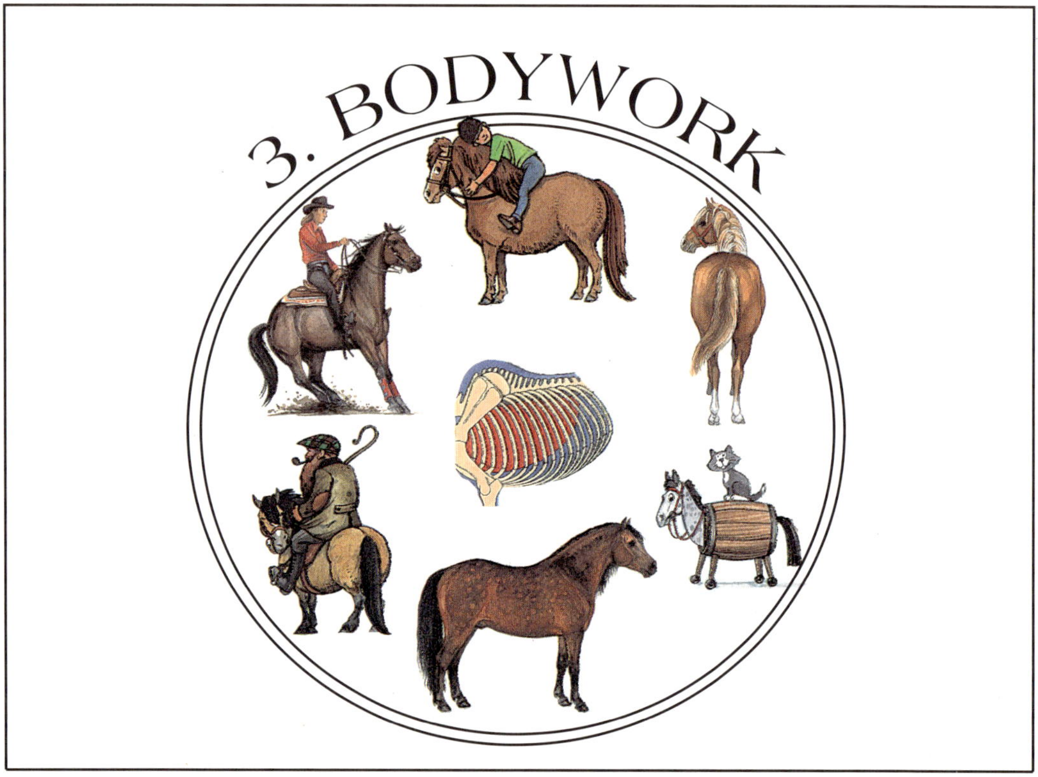